Brunch Done Right: 50 Recipes for Lazy Mornings

By: Kelly Johnson

Table of Contents

- Avocado Toast with Poached Eggs
- Banana Pancakes with Maple Syrup
- Classic French Toast
- Eggs Benedict
- Shakshuka
- Sweet Potato Hash with Fried Eggs
- Croissant Breakfast Sandwiches
- Spinach and Feta Quiche
- Cinnamon Rolls
- Chia Pudding with Fresh Berries
- Breakfast Burrito
- Smoked Salmon and Cream Cheese Bagel
- Omelet with Roasted Veggies
- Pancake Tacos with Bacon
- Scones with Jam and Clotted Cream
- Overnight Oats with Almond Butter
- Avocado and Tomato Salad with Poached Egg
- Baked Avocado Eggs
- Blueberry Muffins
- Granola Parfait
- French Toast Casserole
- Savory Breakfast Muffins
- Churros with Hot Chocolate
- Fruit Salad with Honey-Lime Dressing
- Waffle Bar with Toppings
- Breakfast Pizza
- Ricotta and Honey Toast
- Crêpes with Nutella and Strawberries
- Breakfast Quesadilla
- Poached Eggs on Sweet Potato Toast
- Mushroom and Spinach Frittata
- Ricotta Pancakes with Lemon Zest
- Breakfast Smoothie Bowl
- Bacon and Egg Croissant
- Sautéed Kale and Eggs

- Vegan Breakfast Tacos
- Smoked Salmon Benedict
- Sweet Ricotta and Berry Crepes
- Baked French Toast Sticks
- Egg and Cheese Breakfast Skillet
- Potato Waffles with Avocado
- Ham and Cheese Scones
- Strawberry Shortcake Pancakes
- Maple Bacon Cinnamon Rolls
- Nutella-Stuffed Waffles
- Peaches and Cream Pancakes
- Apple Cinnamon Baked Oatmeal
- Caramelized Onion and Goat Cheese Quiche
- Toasted Bagels with Lox and Capers
- Peach Melba Parfait

Avocado Toast with Poached Eggs

Ingredients:

- 2 slices of bread, toasted
- 1 ripe avocado, mashed
- 2 large eggs, poached
- Salt and pepper, to taste
- Red pepper flakes (optional)

Instructions:

1. **Toast bread** – Toast the bread slices to your desired crispness.
2. **Mash avocado** – Spread mashed avocado on the toasted bread, season with salt and pepper.
3. **Poach eggs** – Poach the eggs in simmering water for 3–4 minutes.
4. **Assemble** – Place poached eggs on top of avocado toast, sprinkle with red pepper flakes if desired, and serve.

Banana Pancakes with Maple Syrup

Ingredients:

- 1 ripe banana, mashed
- 1 cup all-purpose flour
- 1 tbsp sugar
- 1 tsp baking powder
- 1 large egg
- ½ cup milk
- 1 tsp vanilla extract
- Maple syrup for serving

Instructions:

1. **Mix ingredients** – Combine flour, sugar, baking powder, mashed banana, egg, milk, and vanilla in a bowl.
2. **Cook pancakes** – Heat a griddle or skillet over medium heat, grease lightly, and pour batter to form pancakes.
3. **Serve** – Cook until bubbles form, then flip and cook the other side. Serve with maple syrup.

Classic French Toast

Ingredients:

- 4 slices of bread
- 2 large eggs
- ½ cup milk
- 1 tbsp sugar
- ½ tsp cinnamon
- 1 tsp vanilla extract
- Butter for cooking

Instructions:

1. **Whisk batter** – In a bowl, whisk eggs, milk, sugar, cinnamon, and vanilla.
2. **Dip bread** – Soak bread slices in the egg mixture.
3. **Cook** – Heat butter in a pan and cook each side of the bread until golden brown.
4. **Serve** – Serve with syrup or fruit.

Eggs Benedict

Ingredients:

- 2 English muffins, split and toasted
- 4 large eggs, poached
- 4 slices of Canadian bacon
- 1 tbsp white vinegar
- ½ cup hollandaise sauce (homemade or store-bought)
- Chopped chives (optional)

Instructions:

1. **Poach the eggs** – Simmer water with vinegar and gently crack the eggs into the water, cooking for 3–4 minutes.
2. **Cook the bacon** – Brown the Canadian bacon in a skillet.
3. **Assemble** – Place the bacon on the toasted muffin halves, top with poached eggs, and drizzle with hollandaise sauce.
4. **Garnish and serve** – Sprinkle with chives if desired.

Shakshuka

Ingredients:

- 1 can (14 oz) diced tomatoes
- 1 onion, diced
- 2 garlic cloves, minced
- 1 tsp cumin
- ½ tsp paprika
- ½ tsp chili flakes (optional)
- 4 large eggs
- 2 tbsp olive oil
- Fresh parsley for garnish

Instructions:

1. **Sauté onion and garlic** – Cook onion and garlic in olive oil until softened.
2. **Add spices and tomatoes** – Stir in cumin, paprika, and chili flakes, followed by diced tomatoes. Simmer for 10 minutes.
3. **Poach eggs** – Create small wells in the sauce, crack eggs into each, and cook until the eggs are set.
4. **Serve** – Garnish with fresh parsley and serve with warm bread.

Sweet Potato Hash with Fried Eggs

Ingredients:

- 2 medium sweet potatoes, diced
- 1 red bell pepper, diced
- 1 onion, diced
- 2 tbsp olive oil
- 2 large eggs
- Salt and pepper, to taste
- Fresh cilantro (optional)

Instructions:

1. **Cook sweet potatoes** – Heat olive oil in a skillet and cook the sweet potatoes until tender.
2. **Add veggies** – Add onion and bell pepper, cook until softened.
3. **Fry eggs** – In another pan, fry eggs to your liking.
4. **Assemble** – Serve the hash topped with fried eggs and garnish with cilantro.

Croissant Breakfast Sandwiches

Ingredients:

- 2 croissants, split
- 4 large eggs
- 2 slices of cheese (cheddar or Swiss)
- 2 slices of cooked bacon or sausage patties
- Salt and pepper, to taste

Instructions:

1. **Cook eggs** – Scramble or fry eggs and season with salt and pepper.
2. **Assemble sandwiches** – Layer scrambled eggs, cheese, and bacon or sausage on the bottom half of each croissant.
3. **Serve** – Top with the other half of the croissant and serve warm.

Spinach and Feta Quiche

Ingredients:

- 1 pre-made pie crust
- 4 large eggs
- 1 cup heavy cream
- 1 cup spinach, chopped
- ½ cup crumbled feta cheese
- Salt and pepper, to taste

Instructions:

1. **Preheat oven** – Set to 375°F (190°C).
2. **Prepare filling** – Whisk eggs, cream, and seasonings, then add spinach and feta.
3. **Bake** – Pour the mixture into the pie crust and bake for 35–40 minutes, until set.

Cinnamon Rolls

Ingredients:

- 2 ½ cups all-purpose flour
- ¼ cup sugar
- 2 tsp active dry yeast
- 1 cup warm milk
- 1/4 cup butter, softened
- 1 tsp cinnamon
- ½ cup brown sugar
- 1 cup powdered sugar (for icing)

Instructions:

1. **Prepare dough** – Mix flour, sugar, yeast, and warm milk. Let rise for 1 hour.
2. **Roll and fill** – Roll dough into a rectangle, spread with butter, cinnamon, and brown sugar.
3. **Shape rolls** – Roll up dough, slice into pieces, and place in a greased pan. Let rise for 30 minutes.
4. **Bake** – Bake at 350°F (175°C) for 25–30 minutes.
5. **Icing** – Mix powdered sugar with a little milk, drizzle over rolls, and serve.

Chia Pudding with Fresh Berries

Ingredients:

- ¼ cup chia seeds
- 1 cup almond milk (or any milk of choice)
- 1 tbsp honey or maple syrup
- ½ tsp vanilla extract
- Fresh berries (strawberries, blueberries, etc.)

Instructions:

1. **Prepare pudding** – In a bowl, mix chia seeds, almond milk, honey, and vanilla extract.
2. **Refrigerate** – Cover and refrigerate overnight or for at least 4 hours.
3. **Serve** – Top with fresh berries before serving.

Breakfast Burrito

Ingredients:

- 2 large eggs, scrambled
- 1 flour tortilla
- ¼ cup shredded cheese
- 2 tbsp salsa
- ¼ cup cooked bacon or sausage
- ¼ avocado, sliced

Instructions:

1. **Cook eggs** – Scramble the eggs in a pan.
2. **Assemble burrito** – On the tortilla, add scrambled eggs, cheese, salsa, bacon or sausage, and avocado.
3. **Wrap and serve** – Roll up the burrito and serve warm.

Smoked Salmon and Cream Cheese Bagel

Ingredients:

- 1 bagel, halved and toasted
- 2 oz smoked salmon
- 2 tbsp cream cheese
- Fresh dill (optional)
- Red onion, thinly sliced (optional)

Instructions:

1. **Prepare bagel** – Spread cream cheese on each half of the toasted bagel.
2. **Assemble** – Layer smoked salmon on top of the cream cheese.
3. **Garnish** – Add red onion and dill for extra flavor, then serve.

Omelet with Roasted Veggies

Ingredients:

- 3 large eggs
- ½ cup roasted vegetables (e.g., bell peppers, zucchini, tomatoes)
- ¼ cup shredded cheese (optional)
- Salt and pepper, to taste

Instructions:

1. **Cook eggs** – Whisk eggs and cook in a nonstick skillet until slightly set.
2. **Add veggies** – Add roasted veggies and cheese (if using) to one half of the omelet.
3. **Fold and serve** – Fold the omelet in half and serve warm.

Pancake Tacos with Bacon

Ingredients:

- 4 small pancakes
- 4 slices of cooked bacon
- 2 scrambled eggs
- Maple syrup, for drizzling

Instructions:

1. **Assemble tacos** – Place scrambled eggs and bacon slices in the center of each pancake.
2. **Fold** – Fold pancakes like tacos.
3. **Serve** – Drizzle with maple syrup and enjoy.

Scones with Jam and Clotted Cream

Ingredients:

- 2 cups all-purpose flour
- 1 tbsp baking powder
- 1/3 cup sugar
- 6 tbsp cold butter
- 1 large egg
- 2/3 cup milk
- Jam and clotted cream, for serving

Instructions:

1. **Preheat oven** – Set to 375°F (190°C) and line a baking sheet with parchment paper.
2. **Prepare dough** – Mix flour, baking powder, and sugar, then cut in butter. Add egg and milk, stir until combined.
3. **Shape and bake** – Pat dough into a circle, cut into wedges, and bake for 15–20 minutes.
4. **Serve** – Serve warm with jam and clotted cream.

Overnight Oats with Almond Butter

Ingredients:

- ½ cup rolled oats
- 1 cup almond milk (or any milk of choice)
- 1 tbsp almond butter
- 1 tsp honey or maple syrup
- Fresh fruit for topping (optional)

Instructions:

1. **Prepare oats** – Mix oats, almond milk, almond butter, and honey in a jar or bowl.
2. **Refrigerate** – Cover and refrigerate overnight.
3. **Serve** – Top with fresh fruit in the morning and enjoy.

Avocado and Tomato Salad with Poached Egg

Ingredients:

- 1 ripe avocado, sliced
- 1 tomato, diced
- 2 large eggs, poached
- Olive oil, for drizzling
- Salt and pepper, to taste
- Fresh basil for garnish (optional)

Instructions:

1. **Prepare salad** – Arrange avocado slices and diced tomatoes on a plate.
2. **Poach eggs** – Poach eggs in simmering water for 3–4 minutes.
3. **Assemble** – Place poached eggs on top of the salad, drizzle with olive oil, and season with salt and pepper.
4. **Serve** – Garnish with fresh basil if desired.

Baked Avocado Eggs

Ingredients:

- 2 ripe avocados
- 4 large eggs
- Salt and pepper, to taste
- Fresh herbs (optional)

Instructions:

1. **Preheat oven** – Set to 375°F (190°C).
2. **Prepare avocados** – Cut avocados in half and remove the pit. Scoop out a little flesh to make room for the egg.
3. **Add eggs** – Crack an egg into each avocado half.
4. **Bake** – Place on a baking sheet and bake for 12–15 minutes, until eggs are set.
5. **Serve** – Season with salt and pepper, garnish with herbs if desired, and enjoy warm.

Blueberry Muffins

Ingredients:

- 1 ½ cups all-purpose flour
- ½ cup sugar
- 1 tbsp baking powder
- ½ tsp salt
- 1/3 cup milk
- 1/3 cup vegetable oil
- 1 large egg
- 1 cup fresh or frozen blueberries

Instructions:

1. **Preheat oven** – Set to 375°F (190°C) and line a muffin tin with paper liners.
2. **Mix dry ingredients** – Combine flour, sugar, baking powder, and salt in a bowl.
3. **Mix wet ingredients** – Whisk together milk, oil, and egg.
4. **Combine and fold** – Add wet ingredients to dry, then fold in blueberries gently.
5. **Bake** – Fill muffin cups and bake for 18–20 minutes.

Granola Parfait

Ingredients:

- 1 cup granola
- 1 cup Greek yogurt
- 1 cup mixed fresh berries (strawberries, blueberries, raspberries)
- Honey for drizzling (optional)

Instructions:

1. **Layer parfait** – In a glass or jar, layer granola, yogurt, and berries.
2. **Repeat layers** – Add additional layers until the jar is filled.
3. **Top and serve** – Drizzle with honey if desired and serve chilled.

French Toast Casserole

Ingredients:

- 8 slices of bread, cubed
- 4 large eggs
- 2 cups milk
- 1 tsp vanilla extract
- ½ tsp cinnamon
- ¼ cup maple syrup

Instructions:

1. **Preheat oven** – Set to 350°F (175°C).
2. **Prepare casserole** – Layer cubed bread in a greased baking dish.
3. **Mix eggs and milk** – Whisk eggs, milk, vanilla, and cinnamon. Pour over bread cubes and let it soak for 10 minutes.
4. **Bake** – Drizzle with maple syrup and bake for 35–40 minutes, until golden.

Savory Breakfast Muffins

Ingredients:

- 1 ½ cups all-purpose flour
- 1 tbsp baking powder
- ½ tsp salt
- 1/3 cup milk
- 1/3 cup olive oil
- 1 large egg
- 1/2 cup cooked bacon or sausage, crumbled
- ½ cup shredded cheese (cheddar or feta)

Instructions:

1. **Preheat oven** – Set to 375°F (190°C) and line a muffin tin with paper liners.
2. **Mix dry ingredients** – Combine flour, baking powder, and salt.
3. **Mix wet ingredients** – Whisk together milk, oil, and egg.
4. **Combine and fold** – Add wet ingredients to dry, then fold in bacon or sausage and cheese.
5. **Bake** – Fill muffin cups and bake for 18–20 minutes.

Churros with Hot Chocolate

Ingredients:

- 1 cup water
- 1 tbsp sugar
- 1 tsp vanilla extract
- 1 ½ cups all-purpose flour
- 2 tbsp butter
- ½ tsp salt
- 1 egg
- 2 cups oil for frying
- ½ cup sugar for coating
- ¼ tsp cinnamon

Instructions:

1. **Make dough** – Bring water, sugar, vanilla, butter, and salt to a boil. Stir in flour and cook until it forms a dough. Let it cool, then mix in the egg.
2. **Fry churros** – Heat oil in a deep pan. Pipe dough into the oil and fry until golden brown.
3. **Coat churros** – Toss churros in a cinnamon-sugar mixture.
4. **Serve with chocolate** – Serve with a cup of hot chocolate for dipping.

Fruit Salad with Honey-Lime Dressing

Ingredients:

- 2 cups mixed fresh fruit (melon, berries, pineapple, etc.)
- 2 tbsp honey
- 1 tbsp lime juice
- Fresh mint for garnish (optional)

Instructions:

1. **Prepare fruit** – Cut the fruit into bite-sized pieces and place in a bowl.
2. **Make dressing** – Mix honey and lime juice in a small bowl.
3. **Combine** – Drizzle dressing over fruit and toss gently.
4. **Serve** – Garnish with fresh mint and serve chilled.

Waffle Bar with Toppings

Ingredients:

- Waffle batter (store-bought or homemade)
- Assorted toppings:
    - Fresh berries
    - Maple syrup
    - Whipped cream
    - Chocolate chips
    - Nut butter
    - Sliced bananas
    - Chopped nuts

Instructions:

1. **Cook waffles** – Prepare waffles according to package or recipe instructions.
2. **Set up toppings** – Arrange toppings in small bowls for easy access.
3. **Serve** – Allow everyone to build their own waffles with their favorite toppings.

Breakfast Pizza

Ingredients:

- 1 pizza dough (store-bought or homemade)
- 4 large eggs
- ½ cup shredded mozzarella cheese
- ¼ cup cooked bacon or sausage
- 1 tbsp olive oil
- Salt and pepper, to taste

Instructions:

1. **Preheat oven** – Set to 425°F (220°C).
2. **Prepare pizza** – Roll out pizza dough onto a baking sheet, drizzle with olive oil, and sprinkle with mozzarella.
3. **Add toppings** – Create small wells in the dough and crack eggs into them. Add cooked bacon or sausage.
4. **Bake** – Bake for 12–15 minutes until eggs are set.
5. **Serve** – Season with salt and pepper, and serve warm.

Ricotta and Honey Toast

Ingredients:

- 2 slices of bread, toasted
- ¼ cup ricotta cheese
- 1 tbsp honey
- Fresh fruit (optional, for topping)

Instructions:

1. **Toast bread** – Toast the bread slices until golden.
2. **Spread ricotta** – Spread a generous layer of ricotta on each slice.
3. **Drizzle with honey** – Drizzle honey over the ricotta and top with fresh fruit if desired.
4. **Serve** – Enjoy immediately for a sweet breakfast or snack.

Crêpes with Nutella and Strawberries

Ingredients:

- 1 cup all-purpose flour
- 2 large eggs
- 1 ¼ cups milk
- 1 tbsp sugar
- ½ tsp vanilla extract
- ½ cup Nutella
- Fresh strawberries, sliced

Instructions:

1. **Prepare crêpe batter** – Whisk flour, eggs, milk, sugar, and vanilla until smooth.
2. **Cook crêpes** – Heat a nonstick pan, pour in a thin layer of batter, and cook until lightly golden on each side.
3. **Assemble** – Spread Nutella on each crêpe and add sliced strawberries.
4. **Serve** – Roll or fold crêpes and serve warm.

Breakfast Quesadilla

Ingredients:

- 2 large flour tortillas
- 2 scrambled eggs
- ½ cup shredded cheese
- ¼ cup cooked sausage or bacon
- Salsa (optional)

Instructions:

1. **Cook eggs** – Scramble eggs in a pan until set.
2. **Assemble quesadilla** – Place one tortilla in a skillet, layer with scrambled eggs, cheese, and sausage. Top with the second tortilla.
3. **Cook** – Cook each side for 3–4 minutes, until golden and crispy.
4. **Serve** – Slice and serve with salsa if desired.

Poached Eggs on Sweet Potato Toast

Ingredients:

- 1 large sweet potato, sliced into ½-inch thick slices
- 2 large eggs
- Salt and pepper, to taste
- Olive oil, for drizzling

Instructions:

1. **Toast sweet potato** – Heat a griddle or oven to 400°F (200°C). Drizzle sweet potato slices with olive oil and bake for 20 minutes, flipping halfway through.
2. **Poach eggs** – Poach eggs in simmering water for 3–4 minutes.
3. **Assemble** – Place poached eggs on sweet potato toast and season with salt and pepper.
4. **Serve** – Enjoy immediately for a healthy, savory breakfast.

Mushroom and Spinach Frittata

Ingredients:

- 6 large eggs
- 1 cup spinach, chopped
- 1 cup mushrooms, sliced
- 1/2 cup grated cheese (optional)
- Salt and pepper, to taste
- 1 tbsp olive oil

Instructions:

1. **Preheat oven** – Set to 375°F (190°C).
2. **Cook mushrooms** – Sauté mushrooms in olive oil until tender, then add spinach and cook until wilted.
3. **Prepare frittata** – Whisk eggs with salt, pepper, and cheese, then pour over the veggies in the pan.
4. **Bake** – Transfer to the oven and bake for 15–20 minutes until eggs are set.
5. **Serve** – Slice and serve warm for breakfast or brunch.

Ricotta Pancakes with Lemon Zest

Ingredients:

- 1 cup ricotta cheese
- 1 cup all-purpose flour
- 2 large eggs
- 1 tsp baking powder
- ½ cup milk
- Zest of 1 lemon
- 2 tbsp sugar

Instructions:

1. **Prepare batter** – In a bowl, mix ricotta, eggs, milk, lemon zest, flour, baking powder, and sugar until smooth.
2. **Cook pancakes** – Heat a nonstick pan, ladle in batter, and cook until bubbles form, then flip and cook until golden.
3. **Serve** – Top with fresh fruit, syrup, or powdered sugar for a refreshing breakfast.

Breakfast Smoothie Bowl

Ingredients:

- 1 frozen banana
- ½ cup frozen mixed berries
- ½ cup Greek yogurt
- ¼ cup almond milk
- Granola and fresh fruit for topping

Instructions:

1. **Blend ingredients** – In a blender, combine frozen banana, berries, yogurt, and almond milk. Blend until smooth and thick.
2. **Serve** – Pour into a bowl and top with granola, fresh fruit, and any other desired toppings.

Bacon and Egg Croissant

Ingredients:

- 1 large croissant, split
- 2 slices of bacon, cooked
- 1 large egg
- 1 slice cheese (optional)

Instructions:

1. **Cook bacon and egg** – Fry bacon and cook the egg to your preference.
2. **Assemble croissant** – Place cooked bacon and egg inside the croissant, adding cheese if desired.
3. **Serve** – Enjoy warm as a quick and delicious breakfast sandwich.

Sautéed Kale and Eggs

Ingredients:

- 2 large eggs
- 1 bunch kale, stems removed and chopped
- 1 tbsp olive oil
- 1 garlic clove, minced
- Salt and pepper, to taste

Instructions:

1. **Sauté kale** – Heat olive oil in a pan, add garlic, and sauté until fragrant. Add kale and cook until wilted.
2. **Cook eggs** – In a separate pan, fry eggs to your liking.
3. **Assemble** – Serve eggs on top of sautéed kale and season with salt and pepper.
4. **Serve** – Enjoy this nutritious, veggie-packed breakfast!

Vegan Breakfast Tacos

Ingredients:

- 2 small corn tortillas
- ½ cup black beans, cooked
- 1 small avocado, sliced
- 1 medium tomato, diced
- 1 small red onion, diced
- 2 tbsp fresh cilantro, chopped
- Salsa (optional)
- Lime wedges for garnish

Instructions:

1. **Warm tortillas** – Heat the tortillas in a dry skillet or on a griddle.
2. **Assemble tacos** – Layer black beans, avocado slices, diced tomato, red onion, and cilantro on each tortilla.
3. **Serve** – Top with salsa and serve with a lime wedge for extra flavor.

Smoked Salmon Benedict

Ingredients:

- 2 English muffins, split and toasted
- 4 oz smoked salmon
- 4 large eggs, poached
- ½ cup hollandaise sauce (homemade or store-bought)
- Fresh dill for garnish (optional)

Instructions:

1. **Poach the eggs** – Gently simmer water with a little vinegar and poach the eggs until set.
2. **Assemble** – Place a slice of smoked salmon on each half of the toasted English muffins.
3. **Top with eggs** – Place a poached egg on top of the salmon, then drizzle with hollandaise sauce.
4. **Garnish and serve** – Sprinkle with fresh dill if desired and serve immediately.

Sweet Ricotta and Berry Crepes

Ingredients:

- 1 cup all-purpose flour
- 2 large eggs
- 1 ¼ cups almond milk
- 1 tbsp sugar
- 1 tsp vanilla extract
- 1 cup ricotta cheese
- 1 tbsp honey or maple syrup
- Fresh mixed berries (strawberries, blueberries, raspberries)

Instructions:

1. **Prepare crepe batter** – Whisk flour, eggs, almond milk, sugar, and vanilla until smooth.
2. **Cook crepes** – Heat a nonstick pan and pour a small amount of batter, cooking each crepe until golden brown on both sides.
3. **Prepare filling** – In a bowl, mix ricotta with honey or maple syrup.
4. **Assemble** – Spread ricotta mixture on each crepe and top with fresh berries. Fold and serve.

Baked French Toast Sticks

Ingredients:

- 4 slices of bread, cut into strips
- 2 large eggs
- 1 cup milk
- 1 tsp vanilla extract
- 1 tbsp cinnamon
- 2 tbsp sugar
- Butter for greasing

Instructions:

1. **Preheat oven** – Set to 375°F (190°C) and grease a baking sheet.
2. **Prepare mixture** – In a bowl, whisk eggs, milk, vanilla, cinnamon, and sugar.
3. **Dip bread** – Dip bread strips into the egg mixture and place on the baking sheet.
4. **Bake** – Bake for 15–20 minutes, flipping halfway through. Serve with syrup or powdered sugar.

Egg and Cheese Breakfast Skillet

Ingredients:

- 4 large eggs
- 1 cup shredded cheese (cheddar or mozzarella)
- 1 small potato, diced
- ½ cup bell peppers, diced
- ¼ cup onion, diced
- 1 tbsp olive oil
- Salt and pepper, to taste

Instructions:

1. **Cook potatoes** – Heat olive oil in a skillet and cook diced potatoes until golden and crispy.
2. **Add veggies** – Stir in bell peppers and onion, cooking until soft.
3. **Cook eggs** – Create wells in the mixture and crack eggs into each well. Cook to desired doneness.
4. **Top with cheese** – Sprinkle cheese over the eggs and cook until melted.
5. **Serve** – Season with salt and pepper and serve hot.

Potato Waffles with Avocado

Ingredients:

- 2 cups mashed potatoes (cooled)
- 1 cup all-purpose flour
- 1 tsp baking powder
- 1 tbsp olive oil
- Salt and pepper, to taste
- 1 ripe avocado, sliced
- Lime wedges for garnish

Instructions:

1. **Preheat waffle maker** – Heat to medium-high.
2. **Prepare batter** – In a bowl, combine mashed potatoes, flour, baking powder, olive oil, salt, and pepper.
3. **Cook waffles** – Spoon batter into the waffle maker and cook until golden and crispy.
4. **Serve** – Top with sliced avocado and serve with lime wedges.

Ham and Cheese Scones

Ingredients:

- 2 cups all-purpose flour
- 1 tbsp baking powder
- ½ tsp salt
- ½ cup cold butter, cubed
- ½ cup grated cheese (cheddar or Swiss)
- ½ cup diced ham
- ½ cup milk
- 1 large egg (for brushing)

Instructions:

1. **Preheat oven** – Set to 400°F (200°C) and line a baking sheet with parchment paper.
2. **Prepare dough** – In a bowl, mix flour, baking powder, and salt. Cut in butter until the mixture resembles coarse crumbs. Add cheese, ham, and milk, stirring until just combined.
3. **Shape and bake** – Form dough into a circle, cut into wedges, and brush with a beaten egg. Bake for 15–18 minutes until golden.

Strawberry Shortcake Pancakes

Ingredients:

- 1 ½ cups all-purpose flour
- 1 tbsp sugar
- 1 tbsp baking powder
- 1 pinch salt
- 1 cup milk
- 1 egg
- 1 tbsp butter, melted
- 1 cup fresh strawberries, sliced
- 2 tbsp sugar (for strawberries)
- Whipped cream for topping

Instructions:

1. **Prepare strawberries** – Toss sliced strawberries with 2 tbsp sugar and let sit for 10 minutes to release juices.
2. **Prepare pancake batter** – Mix flour, sugar, baking powder, salt, milk, egg, and melted butter until smooth.
3. **Cook pancakes** – Heat a nonstick pan and cook pancakes until golden on both sides.
4. **Assemble** – Layer pancakes with strawberries and top with whipped cream.
5. **Serve** – Enjoy a delicious strawberry shortcake-inspired breakfast.

Maple Bacon Cinnamon Rolls

Ingredients:

- 1 can refrigerated cinnamon roll dough
- 6 slices cooked bacon, crumbled
- ¼ cup maple syrup
- 1 tbsp butter, melted

Instructions:

1. **Preheat oven** – Set to 375°F (190°C) and grease a baking pan.
2. **Prepare rolls** – Unroll the cinnamon dough and sprinkle crumbled bacon over the dough. Roll it back up and slice into individual rolls.
3. **Bake** – Place the rolls in the baking pan and bake according to package directions (typically 15–18 minutes).
4. **Prepare glaze** – Mix maple syrup with melted butter, then drizzle over the hot rolls once baked.
5. **Serve** – Enjoy warm with an extra drizzle of syrup if desired.

Nutella-Stuffed Waffles

Ingredients:

- 1 ½ cups waffle mix (or homemade batter)
- 4 tbsp Nutella
- 1 egg
- 1 cup milk
- 2 tbsp melted butter
- Powdered sugar for dusting

Instructions:

1. **Preheat waffle iron** – Heat to medium-high and lightly grease.
2. **Prepare waffle batter** – Mix waffle mix, egg, milk, and melted butter until smooth.
3. **Assemble waffles** – Spoon a little batter into the waffle iron, add a teaspoon of Nutella, then top with more batter.
4. **Cook waffles** – Close the waffle iron and cook until golden and crispy.
5. **Serve** – Dust with powdered sugar and enjoy warm.

Peaches and Cream Pancakes

Ingredients:

- 1 ½ cups pancake mix
- 1 cup milk
- 1 egg
- 1 tsp vanilla extract
- 2 fresh peaches, sliced
- ¼ cup heavy cream
- 1 tbsp powdered sugar

Instructions:

1. **Prepare pancake batter** – Mix pancake mix, milk, egg, and vanilla until smooth.
2. **Cook pancakes** – Pour batter onto a hot griddle and cook until golden on both sides.
3. **Prepare cream** – Whisk heavy cream with powdered sugar until thickened.
4. **Assemble** – Serve pancakes with fresh peach slices and a dollop of whipped cream.
5. **Serve** – Enjoy with syrup if desired!

Apple Cinnamon Baked Oatmeal

Ingredients:

- 2 cups rolled oats
- 1 ½ cups almond milk (or any milk of choice)
- 2 apples, diced
- 1 tsp cinnamon
- ¼ cup maple syrup
- 1 tsp vanilla extract
- 2 tbsp butter, melted
- 1 egg

Instructions:

1. **Preheat oven** – Set to 375°F (190°C) and grease a baking dish.
2. **Mix ingredients** – In a bowl, combine oats, milk, diced apples, cinnamon, maple syrup, vanilla, melted butter, and egg.
3. **Bake** – Pour mixture into the baking dish and bake for 25–30 minutes until set.
4. **Serve** – Top with additional maple syrup or yogurt if desired.

Caramelized Onion and Goat Cheese Quiche

Ingredients:

- 1 pre-made pie crust
- 1 large onion, thinly sliced
- 1 tbsp olive oil
- 4 large eggs
- 1 cup heavy cream
- ¼ cup crumbled goat cheese
- Salt and pepper, to taste

Instructions:

1. **Preheat oven** – Set to 350°F (175°C).
2. **Caramelize onions** – Sauté onions in olive oil over low heat until soft and golden (about 15 minutes).
3. **Prepare filling** – In a bowl, whisk eggs with heavy cream, salt, and pepper. Stir in caramelized onions and goat cheese.
4. **Assemble and bake** – Pour mixture into the pie crust and bake for 35–40 minutes until set and lightly golden.
5. **Serve** – Let cool slightly before slicing and serving.

Toasted Bagels with Lox and Capers

Ingredients:

- 2 bagels, halved
- 4 oz cream cheese
- 4 oz smoked salmon (lox)
- 1 tbsp capers
- 1 small red onion, thinly sliced
- Fresh dill for garnish

Instructions:

1. **Toast bagels** – Toast the bagel halves until crispy and golden.
2. **Spread cream cheese** – Spread a generous layer of cream cheese on each toasted bagel half.
3. **Assemble** – Top with smoked salmon, capers, onion slices, and garnish with fresh dill.
4. **Serve** – Serve immediately for a delicious breakfast or brunch.

Peach Melba Parfait

Ingredients:

- 1 cup fresh peaches, sliced
- 1 cup raspberry jam or fresh raspberries
- 1 cup Greek yogurt
- 2 tbsp honey
- ¼ cup granola

Instructions:

1. **Prepare peaches** – Slice fresh peaches and set aside.
2. **Layer parfait** – In serving glasses, layer Greek yogurt, peach slices, raspberry jam or fresh raspberries, and a drizzle of honey.
3. **Top with granola** – Sprinkle granola on top for crunch.
4. **Serve** – Serve immediately for a fresh, layered parfait breakfast.

www.ingramcontent.com/pod-product-compliance
Lightning Source LLC
LaVergne TN
LVHW081507060526
838201LV00056BA/2991